Rookie biographies®

Helen Keller

By Sean Dolan

Consultant
Nanci R. Vargus, EdD
Assistant Professor of Literacy
University of Indianapolis
Indianapolis, Indiana

Children's Press®
A Division of Scholastic Inc.
New York Toronto London Auckland Sydney
Mexico City New Delhi Hong Kong
Danbury, Connecticut

Designer: Herman Adler Design
Photo Researcher: Caroline Anderson
The photo on the cover shows Helen Keller.

Library of Congress Cataloging-in-Publication Data

Dolan, Sean.
  Helen Keller / by Sean Dolan ; consultant, Nancy R. Vargus.
    p. cm. – (Rookie biographies)
  Includes index.
  ISBN 0-516-25269-0 (lib. bdg.)   0-516-25481-2 (pbk.)
  1. Keller, Helen, 1880–1968–Juvenile literature. 2. Blind-deaf women–United
States—Biography–Juvenile literature. I. Title. II. Series: Rookie biography.
  HV1624.K4D65 2005
  362.4'1'092–dc22   005002106

8 9 10 R 14 13 12   62

Did you know that some people read or talk with their hands?

This teacher is using sign language to talk to her student.

Helen Keller did both!

Keller was born in 1880, in Tuscumbia, Alabama.

When she was a baby, she got very sick. Her sickness left her unable to see or hear.

Her parents were told that she would never be able to learn or communicate. To communicate means to share ideas.

Anne Sullivan became Helen Keller's teacher in 1887.

Keller's parents hired Anne Sullivan. Sullivan knew how to teach Keller.

Sullivan traveled a long way to get to Keller's home in Alabama.

She started teaching Keller right away. She spelled words into Keller's hand.

This is the water pump that Sullivan used to teach Keller the word *water*.

One day, Sullivan spelled the word *water*. Then, she held Keller's hand under some running water.

Sullivan did this over and over.
Keller started to understand.

Keller realized Sullivan was using her fingers to make letters. The letters spelled out words.

Keller began learning a lot of
new things. Sullivan helped
Keller learn how to read
and write.

Helen read by feeling raised dots, called braille.

Keller went to one of the best colleges in the country.

She graduated in 1904.

Keller wrote many books. Her books told the story of her life.

This is a scene from the movie made about Keller's life.

Keller became famous all over
the world.

A play was written about her.
It was made into a movie.

Keller traveled to many countries.

This is Keller in Japan.

Helen Keller met with President John F. Kennedy in 1961.

She met with kings, queens,
and presidents.

Helen Keller died in 1968. She showed people that they can do anything.

Words You Know

Anne Sullivan

braille

graduated

president

teacher

water pump

writing

Index

About the Author

Sean Dolan is a writer, songwriter, and musician. He has written more than thirty biographies for young readers.

Photo Credits

Photographs © 2005: American Foundation for the Blind, Inc.: 4, 26; AP/Wide World Photos: 7, 28; Corbis Images: 12, 16, 19, 24, 30 top right, 31 bottom left (Bettmann), 23, 31 bottom right (Hulton-Deutsch Collection), 15 (UPI), 27, 31 top left; New York Time Studio: cover; Perkins School for the Blind: 8, 11, 30 top left; PhotoEdit/Spencer Grant: 3, 31 top right; Schlesinger Library, Radcliffe College: 20, 30 bottom.